Poems on several occasions. By a lady.

Charlotte Campbell Bury

ECCO
PRINT EDITIONS

Eighteenth Century
Collections Online
Print Editions

Gale ECCO Print Editions

Relive history with *Eighteenth Century Collections Online*, now available in print for the independent historian and collector. This series includes the most significant English-language and foreign-language works printed in Great Britain during the eighteenth century, and is organized in seven different subject areas including literature and language; medicine, science, and technology; and religion and philosophy. The collection also includes thousands of important works from the Americas.

The eighteenth century has been called "The Age of Enlightenment." It was a period of rapid advance in print culture and publishing, in world exploration, and in the rapid growth of science and technology – all of which had a profound impact on the political and cultural landscape. At the end of the century the American Revolution, French Revolution and Industrial Revolution, perhaps three of the most significant events in modern history, set in motion developments that eventually dominated world political, economic, and social life.

In a groundbreaking effort, Gale initiated a revolution of its own: digitization of epic proportions to preserve these invaluable works in the largest online archive of its kind. Contributions from major world libraries constitute over 175,000 original printed works. Scanned images of the actual pages, rather than transcriptions, recreate the works *as they first appeared.*

Now for the first time, these high-quality digital scans of original works are available via print-on-demand, making them readily accessible to libraries, students, independent scholars, and readers of all ages.

For our initial release we have created seven robust collections to form one the world's most comprehensive catalogs of 18th century works.

Initial Gale ECCO Print Editions collections include:

History and Geography
Rich in titles on English life and social history, this collection spans the world as it was known to eighteenth-century historians and explorers. Titles include a wealth of travel accounts and diaries, histories of nations from throughout the world, and maps and charts of a world that was still being discovered. Students of the War of American Independence will find fascinating accounts from the British side of conflict.

Social Science

Delve into what it was like to live during the eighteenth century by reading the first-hand accounts of everyday people, including city dwellers and farmers, businessmen and bankers, artisans and merchants, artists and their patrons, politicians and their constituents. Original texts make the American, French, and Industrial revolutions vividly contemporary.

Medicine, Science and Technology

Medical theory and practice of the 1700s developed rapidly, as is evidenced by the extensive collection, which includes descriptions of diseases, their conditions, and treatments. Books on science and technology, agriculture, military technology, natural philosophy, even cookbooks, are all contained here.

Literature and Language

Western literary study flows out of eighteenth-century works by Alexander Pope, Daniel Defoe, Henry Fielding, Frances Burney, Denis Diderot, Johann Gottfried Herder, Johann Wolfgang von Goethe, and others. Experience the birth of the modern novel, or compare the development of language using dictionaries and grammar discourses.

Religion and Philosophy

The Age of Enlightenment profoundly enriched religious and philosophical understanding and continues to influence present-day thinking. Works collected here include masterpieces by David Hume, Immanuel Kant, and Jean-Jacques Rousseau, as well as religious sermons and moral debates on the issues of the day, such as the slave trade. The Age of Reason saw conflict between Protestantism and Catholicism transformed into one between faith and logic -- a debate that continues in the twenty-first century.

Law and Reference

This collection reveals the history of English common law and Empire law in a vastly changing world of British expansion. Dominating the legal field is the *Commentaries of the Law of England* by Sir William Blackstone, which first appeared in 1765. Reference works such as almanacs and catalogues continue to educate us by revealing the day-to-day workings of society.

Fine Arts

The eighteenth-century fascination with Greek and Roman antiquity followed the systematic excavation of the ruins at Pompeii and Herculaneum in southern Italy; and after 1750 a neoclassical style dominated all artistic fields. The titles here trace developments in mostly English-language works on painting, sculpture, architecture, music, theater, and other disciplines. Instructional works on musical instruments, catalogs of art objects, comic operas, and more are also included.

The BiblioLife Network

This project was made possible in part by the BiblioLife Network (BLN), a project aimed at addressing some of the huge challenges facing book preservationists around the world. The BLN includes libraries, library networks, archives, subject matter experts, online communities and library service providers. We believe every book ever published should be available as a high-quality print reproduction; printed on-demand anywhere in the world. This insures the ongoing accessibility of the content and helps generate sustainable revenue for the libraries and organizations that work to preserve these important materials.

The following book is in the "public domain" and represents an authentic reproduction of the text as printed by the original publisher. While we have attempted to accurately maintain the integrity of the original work, there are sometimes problems with the original work or the micro-film from which the books were digitized. This can result in minor errors in reproduction. Possible imperfections include missing and blurred pages, poor pictures, markings and other reproduction issues beyond our control. Because this work is culturally important, we have made it available as part of our commitment to protecting, preserving, and promoting the world's literature.

GUIDE TO FOLD-OUTS MAPS and OVERSIZED IMAGES

The book you are reading was digitized from microfilm captured over the past thirty to forty years. Years after the creation of the original microfilm, the book was converted to digital files and made available in an online database.

In an online database, page images do not need to conform to the size restrictions found in a printed book. When converting these images back into a printed bound book, the page sizes are standardized in ways that maintain the detail of the original. For large images, such as fold-out maps, the original page image is split into two or more pages

Guidelines used to determine how to split the page image follows:

• Some images are split vertically; large images require vertical and horizontal splits.
• For horizontal splits, the content is split left to right.
• For vertical splits, the content is split from top to bottom.
• For both vertical and horizontal splits, the image is processed from top left to bottom right.

POEMS

ON

SEVERAL OCCASIONS.

POEMS

ON

SEVERAL OCCASIONS.

BY A LADY.

EDINBURGH.

1797.

POEMS

ON

SEVERAL OCCASIONS.

AN ODE TO EVENING.

HIGH on a rocky cliff I ſtand,
O'erhanging far the ſea-beat ſtrand.
Here let me tune my humble lyre;
For ſure, if ought could e'er inſpire,
This hour this ſcene muſt ever prove
Grateful to Poetry and Love.
The eaſtern hills are vail'd in ſhade,
And ſilence now pervades the glade;
Save that with meaſur'd pace each wave
The whiten'd ſands unceaſing lave,
Or that ſome diſtant rural ſound
Echoes among the hills around:

A

But when that found, by foft degrees,

In murmurs mingles with the breeze,

The breeze, which oft to Fancy's ear

Conveys a voice that wakes a tear,

Returning filence fweeter feems,

And raifes fofter, tend'rer dreams.

O'er the fmooth furface of the deep,

Each ruder wind lies hufh'd to fleep:

Through fleecy clouds pale moon-beams glance,

And fwiftly lead their airy dance,

Wand'ring from rocks to woods and vales,

Now filv'ring o'er yon diftant fails,

Which on the main, with crefted pride,

In ftate majeftic flowly glide.

Where the bright fun its courfe did fteer,

There gilded purple clouds appear:

But fee! then colours change and fly,

As Night's grey mantle vails the fky;

True image of our fading joys,

Which every paffing hour deftroys.

Mark to the left, where spreading trees depend,

Whose ancient branches ven'rably bend,

There is a place of rest, where pain will ceafe,

And fublunary ills be lull'd to peace:

Ah! there, perhaps, beneath yon aged stone,

With grafs and ivy now almost o'ergrown,

All that was blefs'd in life lies mould'ring there;

Sad proof how vain our ev'ry worldly care!

Not e'en what coftly marble can proclaim,

Will from oblivion fnatch the hero's fame:

For, like this humble stone, it owns the fway

Of ruthlefs Time, and moulders in decay,

Or foon or late is pafs'd unheeded by,

Nor claims deferved praife, nor Pity's figh

Not fo in heaven. for actions great or fair,

In angels records live immortal there.

From the cold tomb the paffions will retreat,

The throbbing heart will then no longer beat;

For there our fond affections must fubfide,

And death our deareft ties, alas! divide.

Ah! fadd'ning thought, which to defpair controuls

And damps devotion in the pureft fouls,

Go, leave my aching breaft, nor e'er obtrude

A fancied ill fo drear, fo wildly rude,

No, as I view yon azure fpangl'd fky,

Such gloomy images then quickly fly,

And Hope ftill whifpers, that affection's given

To pafs refin'd in happinefs to heaven

Ah! brilliant Hope, celeftial maid!

Without thy ever welcome aid,

Sunk in a dark abyfs of woe,

Uncheer'd, my gloomy days would flow,

But, while illumin'd by thy rays,

Around with placid eye I gaze,

And view each well-known object o'er

That oft has calm'd my mind before.

For like Sol's glowing beams that chafe

Thick vapours from the mountain's face,

Thy bright'ning afpect drives Defpair away,

And fhows through Sorrow's mift a fairer day.

Thofe hills, thefe plains, that cryftal ftream,
Shall ever be my favourite theme
But beft I love yon woods among,
At evening hour to pour my fong;
For there Remembrance fondly dwells,
And every tree fome ftory tells,
That never, fure, can ceafe to be
The fource of tender thought to me:
And there I'll write fuch lays as thefe;
For artlefs lines have pow'r to pleafe.
What though unfkill'd, they yet impart
The foften'd feelings of the heart,
Yielding a penfive, pleafing charm,
That piercing grief can oft difarm,
And mellows to a dulcet tone,
Which Happinefs might call her own.

TO IMPATIENCE

WHY turn to pain a promis'd pleasure,
  By thinking moments long as hours,
Which keeps us from the hop'd-for treasure,
  Too often cloying once 'tis ours.

Ah! let us wisely taste of bliss
  In fondest dreams that Fancy gives,
Nor for possession idly wish ;
  'Tis in our minds each blessing lives.

But weak indeed is Reason's pow'r,
  When Passion throbs thro' all the heart ;
Impatient then it waits the hour
  That will the wish'd-for joy impart.

Philosophy must e'er prove vain
  To calm the tumult Hope endures;
But Reason may at least restrain
  And sooth the pain it never cures.

MORNING

Now Morn appears with aspect gay,
   For spring her step attends ;
But hateful still to me is day :
   'Tis night the wretch befriends.

Ah ! sweet illusions of the night
   Return, and with thee bring
What is more pleasing to my sight
   Than all the charms of spring.

In vain for me those charms appear;
   All Nature blooms in vain ;
But welcome is each vision dear
   Which can beguile my pain.

Thus have I seen some hapless bird
   Its lost companion mourn,
The plaintive note by Echo heard
   Along the waters borne.

The little mourner hears the found
    With rapturous delight,
Now fondly thinks its love is found,
    And quickens now its flight.

Sudden it fees a form appear,
    Reflected in the waves;
But when, alas! it thinks 'tis near,
    His breaft the water laves.

For ftill the luring fhadow flies,
    The fhadow call'd in vain,
Till by degrees the image dies,
    When darknefs vails the main.

Thus all the joys we tafte below,
    Are fhadows in a ftream:
Reality, alas! is woe,
    And Happinefs a dream.

EVENING

Now Evening's vail of fable hue
    Yon diftant hill o'erfpreads,
Tho' Sol's laft beam that's ftill in view
    A trembling luftre fheds.

Here on the nearer vale below,
    The vale with beauty fraught,
It lights the ftream which, murmuring low,
    Awakes the penfive thought.

This is the hour to Fancy kind,
    To fond Remembrance given,
Which calms and elevates the mind,
    And lifts it e'en to Heaven.

Oft at the clofe of fummer days,
    When Nature finks to foft repofe,
My foul with gratitude repays
    The debt of bleffings that it owes.

B

Sure never heart fo callous grown
　　But what muft heave a gentle figh,
And Evening's foothing charm muft own
　　Which fteals the tear from Sorrow's eye.

Sure never heart, that knew to feel
　　Refined enjoyments fuch as thefe,
From fenfibility would fteal
　　One pang to gain infipid eafe.

But if there are who form fuch prayers,
　　And fond extremes would fain refign,
The calm of apathy be theirs,
　　The pleafing pang be always mine.

FALSE and faithlefs as thou art,
Alas ! you ftill poffefs my heart ;
   Nor e'er can time efface
The thought of joys which now are flown,
Tho' with them ev'ry hope is gone,
   Which fooths keen forrow's trace.

Whate'er appearances may be,
In fecret ftill I figh for thee,
   And mourn that I'm forgot :
Thy fragile vows, to me ftill dear,
Are ftill remember'd with a tear,
   But yet, whate'er my lot.

May all thy life with pleafure teem,
May every fun's revolving beam
   Bring health and joy to thee ;
And left remorfe thy heart fhould gain,
Ah ! may you never know the pain
  Which you have caus'd to me.

Where Happinefs, celeftial maid,

With fprightly Fancy ever fway'd

   O'er Sorrow's gloomy power,

There Melancholy fits, confeft

Queen of my foul, for now unbleft

   Is each fad lingering hour.

SONG.

TRANSIENT are the golden fun-beams

   In a varying April day ;

Tranfient all Youth's flattering dreams

   But love is more fo ftill than they.

Go fix the zephyr as it flies,

   Or light that leads the fwain aftray,

Or tints which paint fair fummer fkies,

   As eafy fix'd as love are they.

ON THE SWALLOW.

THE balmy gale of fummer's o'er;

Sweet Philomel enchants no more,

But every drooping flower

Shrinks at th' approach of chilling winds,

And the poor Swallow oft reminds

To fly the wint'ry hour.

Ah ! happy bird ! who feels no pain,

Save from the cold, or beating rain,

Whom innocence makes bleft ;

Who knows no doubts, nor anxious cares,

Whofe breaft no dubious future fears,

Nor jealous pangs moleft.

You feek in warmer climes that blifs,

Which cold deprives you of in this,

And find in change of place

All that you feek ; while I, alas !

Muft through life's various feafons pafs,

Nor hope to find folace.

For ah! no flower which decks the vale,
No perfume wafted with the gale,
   Can case my wounded soul.
They can the happy only please;
Vain are to me such joys as these,
   That ne'er the mind console.

Or if a passing joy they give,
A joy which in a sigh does live,
   And in a tear expires,
It only wakes each painful thought:
The bliss by keen regret is bought,
   With all its vain desires.

Go, then, and taste thy guiltless joys,
Which no remorse or grief alloys;
   Go, leave me to my doom,
To feel the north wind keenly blow,
View the rude mountain torrents flow,
   And woo congenial gloom.

I'll calmly view night's meteor's glare,

While fearful omens flit in air,

　　And mock the tempeſt wild ;

Court the bleak wint'ry howling ſtorm,

Till Fancy paints ſome friendly form,

　　By wiſhes quite beguil'd

A form which then will ſeem to hear

My plaintive tale, and mourn the tear

　　That I am doom'd to ſhed ;

Imagin'd pity ſooths the heart,

And can a ſhort-liv'd joy impart,

　　Though laſting comfort's fled.

Then homewards, penſive, I'll return,

In ſofter accents gently mourn,

　　Weep all paſt pleaſures o'er.

Yet though I am bereft of reſt,

Still gratitude will warm my breaſt :

　　And when the whirlwinds roar,

Then will I wish thee safe, sweet bird!
Thee, whose lov'd voice so oft I've heard
   With transports of delight,
When, gay attendant on the spring,
This way you bent your annual wing,
   And charm'd my infant sight.

By ushering in each early flower,
That oft I pluck'd at evening hour,
   When blest with soft content :
No future care my mind employ'd ;
The present, then, was still enjoy'd,
   And still in blifs was spent.

Far different now the moments fly ;
Reflection heaves th' inceffant sigh,
   And weeps o'er Pleasure's urn :
Now Prudence points out every ill,
Bestows the power, but not the will,
   Her frigid rules to learn.

In vain she beckons from afar,
'Tis like the glim'ring of a star,
 Which breaks beneath a cloud,
So hard her bleffings to obtain,
So fmall proportion'd to the pain,
 Such mifts her brightnefs fhroud.

Like you, my little, harmlefs friend,
Nor courtier I, nor e'er will bend,
 And, fetter'd, not complain.
Let others boaft her magic charm,
Which guards them from all worldly harm ;
 Yet ftill they wear a chain.

No ! I will rather, free as air,
By foft oblivion banifh care,
 Elude misfortune's ftroke.
But, ah ! my filly heart, beware ;
Thy wifh but lures to Fancy's fnare,
 And bids thee own her yoke.

         C

Though sometimes form'd of flow'ry bands,

They fade when touch'd by Sorrow's hands,

   Then sable liv'ries wear,

More fickle than the rainbow's dye,

Like it they change, as quickly fly

   To join their kindred air.

A diff'rent path I must pursue;

A path of thorns, but still in view

   There's Victory crowning Toil.

And meek-ey'd Patience holds the palm,

For ev'ry ill a healing balm,

   That not e'en Time can spoil.

But, gentle Swallow, see yon sky

With gloomy aspect bids thee fly

   To climes where Spring's begun.

Happy's thy lot, compar'd to our's;

For oft Misfortune's cloud that low'rs,

   We see, but cannot shun.

ANSWER

TO " WILT THOU GO WITH ME ?"

YES, I will go with thee, my love,
　And leave all else without a sigh,
Through the wide world with thee I'd rove,
　Nor feel one pang, if thou art nigh.
No coſtly gems, nor courtly ſcenes,
　Have now the ſmalleſt charms for me,
My heart to purer pleaſure leans,
　And all its joys depend on thee.

When far away from natal ſhores,
　And ſeas divide me from each friend,
One look from him my ſoul adores,
　Will courage and freſh vigour lend.
The parching ray, or wintry wind,
　E'en woman's ſoftneſs knows to ſcorn;
True paſſion leaves all fears behind,
　And from the roſe it plucks each thorn

C ij

Then can you doubt my constant love,

    Or can you think I'd fly thy arms?

Ah! give me but the pow'r to prove

    That those are vain, unjust alarms

For sure the flame that gently fann'd

    At first beneath a summer's sky,

Will with redoubled force expand,

    When ruder winds approach it nigh

The lonely cot in desert drear,

    The russet gown and frugal board,

Will greater pleasures far appear,

    Than all that lux'ries here afford

The gay, the busy glitt'ring throng,

    And baneful flatt'ry I'll resign:

To courts and cities these belong,

    But not to Truth and Love like mine

And when, at last, this life is o'er,

    When sickness baffles all my care,

When fairy Hope can cheat no more,
    Then, Cupid, hear thy vot'ry's pray'r
My weeping eyes in pity close,
    E'er they behold my lover's death.
Ah! spare my tears, my hopeless woes,
    And join with his, my parting breath.

ON SEEING SOME WITHERED ROSES THROWN AWAY.

THESE fading flowers too well impart
A mournful leſſon to my heart.
You pluck'd them beauteous, gay and fair,
Their perfume ſcented all the air,
   And fill'd each paſſing gale :
Now withering, languid, almoſt dead,
Their freſhneſs and their beauty fled,
   Their colour ſickly pale.
You throw them with difguſt away,
And as you throw them, ſeem to ſay,
Go, uſeleſs flowers, you pleaſe no more,
Your faſcinating charms are o'er :
   Ah ! what do charms avail !

But had you wiſely kept the flower,
Beyond the limits of an hour,
You might its ſweetneſs have retain'd,
And thence have uſeful morals gain'd,

More eloquent than speech.

Too, ah! full many a fragrant rose
Is lost, through ignorance in those
   That ne'er its merits reach ;
Who ne'er below a surface scann'd,
Pluck flowers with idle, wanton hand ;
And when their beauty once is flown,
To them their ev'ry charm seems gone ;
   But much to me they teach.

For their sad fate, that heart must prove,
Which hopes from thine eternal love,
Allur'd alone by Beauty's power,
Which is impair'd by ev'ry hour,
   Thy love must soon decrease.
Then, Reason, at thy shrine I bow,
Receive a contrite convert now,
   From grief my soul release ;
Oblivion bring to calm the pain,

Else all thy pow'rs will prove but vain ;

Then pluck the dart still rankling here,

Wipe off the yet impassion'd tear,

   And turn my heart to peace

ON SUSPENCE

SOME demon, sure, with vengeful breast,

Envious of joy, and peaceful rest,

Conceiv'd thy all terrific form,

And nursed thee 'mid the wildest storm ;

Where mild content with halcyon eye,

Nor pity's sympathetic sigh,

Then virtues could to thee impart,

Or soften thy obdurate heart.

Furies presided at thy birth,

And sent thee to infest the earth,

Full fraught with ev'ry various ill

Which could their dire resolves fulfil

Thy province is t'embitter life,

To wake the paffions ftill to ftrife,

By fears that blight Hope's opening flower,

And fweeteft bleffings know to four.

The evils which are in thy train

Are greater far than certain pain ;

E'en Sorrow's felf, compar d to thee,

Seems peace and foft tranquillity.

D

A PRAYER

OH Thou! whose power o'er all extends,
   Whom all alike adore,
Low on the dust thy creature bends,
   And dares thy grace implore.

Give to my mind contentment still,
   Whate'er thou mayest ordain,
Let resignation to thy will,
   Sooth e'en severest pain

Make me to think each pang on earth
   Is transient as each joy.
The sun, which gives the floweret birth,
   May soon that flower destroy.

Let me not, therefore, be elate,
   Though Thou should'st bliss bestow;
But teach me never to forget
   From whence those blessings flow

When on this world of trials, Thou
   Almighty power command
To me my fhare, then make me bow
   Submiffive to thy hand.

In beds of fnow the purple flowers
   Their tender bloffoms rear :
The fruitful earth, from winter fhowers,
   Beftows the plenteous year

A feeming ill for real good
   Thy wifdom can ordain ;
So, though by me not underftood,
   Yet may I ne'er complain.

Oh Thou ! who, when the wretched call,
   Lends mercy's gentle ear,
And ev'n ordain'ft a fparrow's fall .——
   Let me not idly fear.

In perils, if I chance to be,
  Though terror ſhould aſſail;
Then may I place my truſt in Thee,
  Who canſt o'er all prevail.

And Thou Omnipotent! who ſees
  The lily in the field,
And from each rude tempeſtuous breeze,
  Who deigns that lily ſhield.

Oh! teach me never to diſdain
  The tears of ſad diſtreſs;
And make me think all pow'r is vain,
  Except the pow'r to bliſs

When others bow beneath the taints,
  Or conſcious bluſh of ſhame,
Then may I ne'er, with fooliſh vaunts,
  My own good deeds proclaim.

To Thee, the Author of all good,
  The praise alone is due,
If e'er temptation is withstood,
  Or if to virtue true.

But, in thy fight, alas! how frail
  Must e'en the best appear;
If mercy did not still prevail,
  I should have all to fear.

So to thy goodness all divine,
  Let me commend my soul,
Oh! make the path of virtue mine;
  My wand'ring steps controul.

And e'er each day's revolving fun
  To worldly cares be given,
May my heart say, Thy will be done,
  O Lord, as 'tis in heaven.

TO THE SHEPHERD OF GLEN.

O'ER rocky mountains, defert glens,
   Yon fhepherd takes his lonely path ;
He neither rapt'rous pleafure kens,
   Nor forrows hath

The dreary hill, the gloomy fky,
   The roaring torrent, white with foam,
Give but th' idea to his eye
   Of native home.

Yon child of Nature's, wildly rude,
   Inur'd to all inclement weather ;
A plaid his raiment, coarfe his food ,
   His bed fome heather.

He afks no trees to fhade his ftream,
   Nor aught to charm his eye ;
Refinements thefe, whofe polifh'd dream
   Ne'er made him figh

He views alike the Summer's fun,
  Alike the Winter's fhower,
And only fays, when day is done,
  My toil is o'er.

Then in his lowly roof'd abode,
  Enjoys the foundeft fleep:
No weeping eyes his reft corrode,
  Nor vigils keep.

As in fome mofs-clad hill he lies,
  I view his peaceful ftate,]
A tear, in vain fupprefs'd, will rife
  To mourn my fate.

Yet all his fhare of happinefs
  From ruftic ign'rance flows;
Refinement would but make it lefs,
  Experience knows.

Happy thou art! then happy be,

    Nor envy me my lot:

Thy ignorance I envy thee,

    And peaceful cot

SONG

WITH dazzling ardour when inflam'd,

All the delights which fancy fram'd

Appear'd within my reach to grow,

The future, then, still met my eye,

Robed in youth's fairest imagery :

But ah ! how soon it chang'd to woe

My eyes were strangers then to tears,

My breast unknown to all those fears

Which teach us soon to dread the morrow;

The smiling hours were ever bright,

Of Time I never mark'd the flight :

But Fancy now is lost in sorrow.

SONG

NOR flighted Love, nor Reafon's fkill,
    Can make foft peace to me return :
Yet to obey thy cruel will,
    Thou never more fhalt hear me mourn.

In fecret I'll indulge my woes,
    And yield to Love's all conqu'ring flame;
But never fhall my lips difclofe
    Th' involuntary fault you blame.

Then let me ftill thy charms behold,
    Still let me view thy angel face ;
For all that's been of Beauty told,
    Thy matchlefs form does fure difgrace.

But if t' admire incurs thy hate,
    Then all alike thou'lt deem thy foe ;
Then fhall I fhare the common fate,
    And thou wilt drown the world in woe.

E

SONG

OR,

DI BACCO SON SEGUACE

Chorus.

Sound the lyre in mirthful strain ;

Let music fill the air ,

The nectar draught of Bacchus drain .

Drink deep, and banish care

IN melting notes of softest measure,

Touch the silver sounding wire,'

And, Cupid, give, to crown all pleasure,

Some sparks of thy celestial fire.

Vain mortals, leave each busy care,

This is the hour of gay delight ;

Come, the Lethean goblet share,

And join to revel out the night.

Ah! grafp the fleeting hours of joy,
   Nor heed whate'er the world may fay;
Time will, too foon, each blifs deftroy:,
   Then catch them ere it flies away.

Still crown thy days with full content,
   Unmindful of the cens'ring throng;
So fhall thy life in joy be fpent,
   All pleafures to content belong.

And fee it fparkles in the bowl,
   Whofe purple juice, each joy can give,
Which warms to mirth the frozen foul,
   And, drown'd in it, 'tis then we live.

Chorus.
Sound the lyre in mirthful ftrain, &c.

E ij

ON BEING ACCUSED OF LEVITY AND INSENSIBILITY.

AH me! full deeply do I know to grieve
    The various ills that life moleft,
My heart's too ready to receive
    Feeling, that fweet, though dang'rous gueft.

When fcenes where diffipation reigns,
    Ceafe to engage each nat'ral thought,
Thoughts which no worldly rule conftrains,
    I loathe all joys which gold e'er bought.

I then, with fighs, defpife each tale,
    That once I try'd to think was fweet;
Then nought do courtly fcenes avail,
    For nature fpeaks in this retreat.

The gawdy crowd, the midnight ball,
    I wonder that I ever fought;
But woods, and lawns, and ftreams recal
    Remembrances with anguifh fraught

Ah! then, far other thoughts enfue,

 To rack my foul with jarring ftrife;

Each foft emotion, then, I rue,

 And fly again to bufy life.

Fly to Ambition's gilded car,

 And own myfelf her willing flave,

Fly from each rural pleafure far,

 For fooner every ftorm I'd brave,

Than thofe which from regret will fpring

 Though reafon tells me they are vain,

While all around confpires to bring

 Inceffant thought of endlefs pain.

For ftill in fecret muft I figh,

 For what I never can obtain,

Unceafing mourn, till mem'ry die,

 That peace which I can ne'er regain

ANSWER TO SOME STANZAS,

B   n i g,

" TO THE ROCKS, STORMS LINDOW, ADIEU."

FROM thefe fhores, how you flew with difdain,

From each fcene which the paft might retrace,

From a heart ftill replete with Affection's fond pain,

Which thy fcorn could not even efface

But I fpeak of the days that are gone,

'Tis a folly I'll try to fubdue,

And what reafon would never have done,

Perchance may be taught me by you :

To bid love an eternal adieu.

It is true I had every fear ,- .

For I lov'd to the utmoft excefs;

Yet, whilft I believ'd you fincere,

I wifh'd not my paffion were lefs.

My heart was Sincerity's felf ,

But alas ! on a bofom fo true,

Thy feigning with eafe could impofe .

By myfelf I too fondly judg'd you,

Who to love had for e'er bade adieu.

But fay not that I could impart

 A charm, which all gloom might difpel,

Nor talk of the hopes of your heart,

 Which only juft bloffom'd and fell.

Thofe pangs and that pleafure were mine,

 That pleafure which tranfiently flew ·

But the pain will for ever remain

 In my heart, which is tender and true,

 E'en when I have bade love adieu.

When I thought myfelf blefs'd with your love,

 Then no threats nor misfortunes I fear'd,

And each hour as it fled, feem'd to prove,

 That by time thou wert only endear'd.

But now the illufion is o'er,

 And thofe hopes that luxuriantly grew

Are flaccid, and drooping, or dead ;

 Ah ! who can then vigour renew ?

 Now you've bade love a final adieu.

Yes, I see yon sea-fowl as it flies

   O'er the waves, while they furiously roll ;

Now it droops, and now struggles to rise .

   'Tis an emblem of my troubled soul.

Through an ocean of sorrow I seek

   An asylum from Love and from you ;

For my heart must or conquer or break :

   But the olive of peace is in view,

   Love, take my last sigh, my adieu.

STANZAS TO THE MOON,

WRITTEN THE LAST EVENING OF THE YEAR 1795.

SAY, beauteous orb, who to a lover's woe
   So oft haft lent sweet visionary bliss,
Say, wilt thou now on me that boon bestow,
   And deign to hear an artless lay like this?

Oft have congenial hearts, though distant far,
   Exchang'd fond wishes in thy love-fraught beams;
For thought of time and space o'erleaps each bar,
   And Misery finds relief in Fancy's dreams.

Oft-times thy silver shedding rays among,
   In sweet illusion kindred souls have join'd,
When tender Sympathy's enchanting tongue
   Speaks the fond language of the mutual mind.

As on thy soft'ning light, serenely bright,
   I've frequent gaz'd, while thought engender'd thought,
My soul to purer regions wing'd its flight,
   And long lost Peace in calm devotion sought.

F

Ah ! who can paint th' ideas which arife,
  As polifh'd minds thy gentle radiance view,
When gliding calmly through unclouded fkies,
  Thy trembling rays illume the glitt'ring dew ?

Or piercing through fome foreft's fombre gloom,
  Beam faintly o'er the leaves of varied dye ;
Or glimmering fweetly on fome ruftic tomb,
  Call from the tender moralift a figh.

Then do I love in lonely fcenes to ftray,
  Where I may chance my penfive mufe to meet,
And joy t' explore fome yet untrodden way,
  While Fancy charms me with her converfe fweet.

'Tis then I can enjoy exiftence beft;
  Each groffer paffion of the mortal frame,
By ev'ning's tranquil foothings lull'd to reft,
  Leaves the pure foul its kindred heaven to claim.

For Cynthia, when thy fweet rays mildly fhine,
    When thought-infpiring ftillnefs reigns around
'Tis then thy tranquil charms, ferene, divine,
    Have calm'd the anguifh of my bofom's wound;

Have taught me then to breathe no murm'ring plaints,
    But grateful be for what kind Heaven beftows :
'Tis Difcontent Enjoyment's bloffom taints,
    And blights each bud of joy ere yet it blows.

But to fupprefs the tributary tear
    Which Mem'ry pays to dear departed blifs,
I ne'er fhall learn fuch fortitude I fear,
    And Virtue's felf can't deem the fear amifs.

For now, alas ! with alter'd eyes I fee,
    And e'en thy beams have loft their wonted power,
Dark, dread fufpenfe dwells, Cynthia, even in thee,
    Adding frefh pangs to ev'ry mournful hour.

I ij

Ah! whilſt I view thy charms, Night's lovely queen,
 How my heart counts each fond remembrance o'er,
And ſwells to burſting, as it paints each ſcene,
 Which now is paſt, and may return no more

Yet lurking Hope ſtill hangs about my ſoul,
 Still kindly flatters with her Syren voice;
A voice which can Deſpair's fell powers controul,
 And bid the drooping heart again rejoice.

Whilſt I behold thee, Cynthia, chaſtly ſhine,
 Ev'n now, perhaps my ſoul's lov'd idol ſhares
The nameleſs pangs which even with Hope entwine
 The tender wiſhes and the anxious cares.

Delightful thought! thou canſt beſtow relief,
 And harmonize Suſpicion's jarring chord,
Which vibrates harſhly to the touch of grief,
 And gives more anguiſh than it e'er can ward.

O thou fair silver orb ! who oft hast heard
    The thousand secret constant vows I've made,
And known the prayers for him to Heaven I've rear'd,
    Say, can such truth by falsehood be repaid ?

Ere from the Morning's sun thy charms ye veil,
    And bid the parting year a long adieu ,
Let fond luxurious Grief past joys bewail,
    And at thy silver shrine her rites renew.

Sad bodes my wistful heart with many a tear,
    Religion's flame burns feebly in my breast,
Quench'd is the holy flame by Misery's tear,
    And chilling doubts my future hopes arrest.

Reliance droops, as dark'ning mists surround
    Each ray of pleasure that was wont to shine,
With gloomy fancies now my thoughts abound,
    And dread Suspense with all the rest combine.

Ere thou, mild orb, thy nightly courſe reſume,

   The morn ſhall uſher in another year,

Pregnant to me, perhaps, with Sorrow's gloom :

   For ſick'ning Fancy paints the future drear.

Thou wilt return, in equal beauty ſhine,

   My heart, unalter'd, ſhall behold thee ſtill,

But not like thee, my deareſt hopes decline,

   To beam again.   Ah ! no, they never will.

BOUTS RIMEES

'TWOULD lull Attention's ſelf to—ſleep,

And make the drooping Muſes—weep,

To ſee the traſh with which we—fill

The road to fam'd Parnaſſus'—hill.

STANZAS

WRITTEN ON READING HAMMOND'S ELEVENTH ELEGY.

AH! who than me with pang acuter feels
 The various horrors which from war arife?
But oh! 'tis God, not man, that forrow deals,
 And in Affliction's fchool our virtue tries.

Ah! who than me more keenly knows to weep
 The ills which gold, man's foe, unceafing rears?
For it, tho' hated and defpis'd, I fteep
 My fleeplefs couch with Sorrow's heartfelt tears.

But when I think that we are born to woe;
 That life, and all its dreams, are quickly o'er;
Then would my foul each earthly care forego,
 And wing its flight where they can pain no more.

Yet not in gelid apathy enfhrin'd,
 Does my fond heart 'gainft feeling proudly ftrive:
For round it Love has all his chains entwin'd,
 And every nerve is tremblingly alive.

But still methinks the wishes of my heart
    Would never be a life of slothful shame;
Glory with love should ever have a part,
    And all my glory be my lover's fame.

The thirst of honour, not the thirst of gain,
    Should dwell within my chosen hero's breast;
Nor even one wish my fearful bosom stain,
    To barter glorious tears for shameful rest.

And when, if to my arms he should return,
    Rich in fair honour, and in modest worth,
Tho' poor in gold, the dross I'd proudly spurn,
    Yet find with him a paradise on earth.

Then would chaste Reason, with a ray serene,
    E'en add fresh charms to those which Love can give,
Still with true pleasure paint life's changing scene,
    And make our virtuous joys immortal live.

THE END

CPSIA information can be obtained
at www.ICGtesting.com
Printed in the USA
LVHW101446270420
654534LV00021B/1303

9 781170 362075